NATIONAL GEOGRAPHIC

T0303065

The Golden Gate Bridge

Rachel Griffiths and Margaret Clyne

Contents

A Spectacular Bridge 3

Who Planned the Golden Gate Bridge? 6

Working Together 8

Why Build a Suspension Bridge? 10

Building the Golden Gate Bridge 14

The Bridge: Past and Present 20

Glossary 23

Index 24

A Spectacular Bridge

The Golden Gate Bridge is one of the most famous and spectacular bridges in the world. Many tourists go to San Francisco, California, just to see the bridge. People know it because of its shape and its orange color.

The bridge has stood through wind, waves, and even earthquakes. It took years to build such a strong bridge. How did the builders make the Golden Gate Bridge so strong?

The Golden Gate Bridge

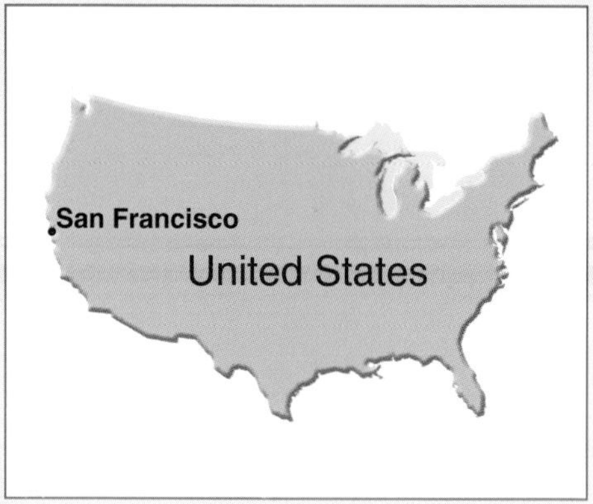

The city of San Francisco sits between the Pacific Ocean and the San Francisco Bay. The city is on a **peninsula**. Water surrounds a peninsula on three sides. A narrow strip of water called the Golden Gate Strait flows between the bay and the ocean.

In the early 1900s, San Francisco was growing into a busy city. More and more people needed to cross the bay. The only way to do this was by boat or ferry. This was slow. And sometimes strong wind, waves, or fog made it dangerous for ferries to cross the bay.

A ferry passes a pier built for the Golden Gate Bridge in 1934.

There had to be a way to cross the Golden Gate Strait. What about a bridge? This bridge would have to be very strong.

Who Planned the Golden Gate Bridge?

Joseph B. Strauss

Some people said the Golden Gate Strait was too long for a bridge. They said the wind or the sea would destroy a bridge. They worried that it would fall down in an earthquake.

Joseph B. Strauss was an **engineer**. An engineer is someone who plans and builds buildings and bridges. Strauss believed that he could build a strong bridge that would cross the Strait. But many people did not like Strauss's first plan. They thought the bridge he planned would be ugly. They wanted a bridge that was as beautiful as the Golden Gate Strait.

So Strauss decided to work with other people to improve his plan. Together they had to draw a new plan that showed a simpler, more beautiful bridge that was also strong and safe.

First, Joseph B. Strauss drew this plan for the Golden Gate Bridge.

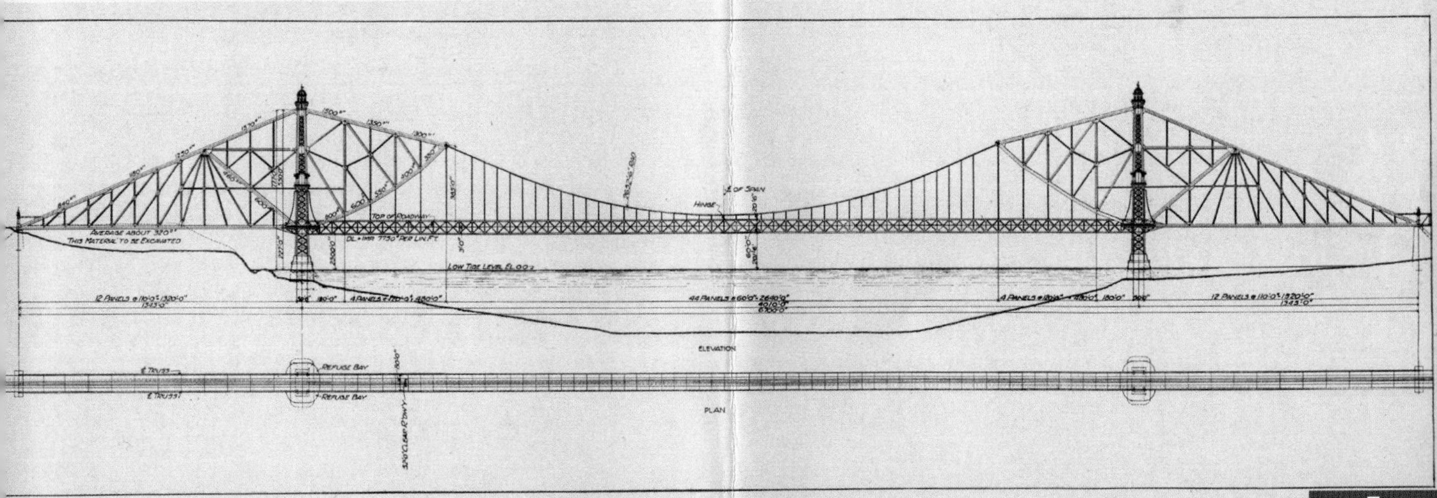

PROPOSED GOLDEN GATE BRIDGE
SIDE ELEVATION AND PLAN

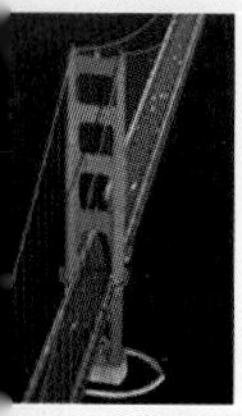

Working Together

Strauss met with other engineers who had many ideas about how to make the bridge strong and beautiful. Strauss and his team did more drawings. They came up with a plan for a bridge that hung from two steel towers.

Joseph B. Strauss (left) and another engineer, Clifford E. Paine, look at the Golden Gate Bridge as it is being built.

Two kinds of **cables**, or strong ropes made of steel, would hold up the roadway. First two long **main cables** would hang across the two towers. Then thinner cables would hang from the two main cables. These cables would hold the roadway. This kind of bridge is called a **suspension bridge**. A suspension bridge this long had never been built before.

Many people liked the plans. They could see that it would be a beautiful bridge. Could Strauss make it strong and safe?

People believed this bridge would be beautiful and strong.

Why Build a Suspension Bridge?

There are many different kinds of bridges. Strauss and his team decided to build a suspension bridge because this bridge can **span**, or cross, long distances. Other kinds of bridges are better for shorter distances.

Suspension bridges are light yet strong. The cables that hang from the towers of a suspension bridge hold most of the bridge's weight. The cables also have to hold the cars and trucks that travel across the bridge.

Cable-stayed bridge

Beam bridge

Arch bridge

People finally agreed that Strauss's suspension bridge would work. Building of this new bridge began in January 1933. This was the start of an exciting time for the people of San Francisco.

Strauss planned to make the bridge very strong and safe by using large amounts of concrete and steel. The concrete would be used to hold the towers and build the **anchorages**. The anchorages are huge blocks that hold the main cables at the end of the bridge.

Did You Know?

The weight of the concrete and steel in each anchorage is 60,000 tons! That's equal to 120 million pounds.

Very hard and heavy concrete was used to build the anchorages.

Anchorage

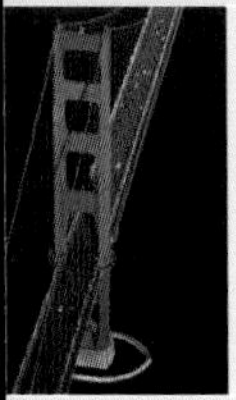

Building the Golden Gate Bridge

First a **pier**, or platform, was built on both sides of the Golden Gate Strait. Each pier would support a steel tower. One pier was built on rock that was close to the shore.

The other pier was harder to build because it had to sit in 110 feet of water. This pier was also far from thc shore.

This picture shows a view of the building from the air. First the pier was built. Then the tower was built on the pier.

When this photo was taken, builders were still working on Tower 1. Tower 2 was finished.

By the end of 1935, after two years, the piers and the two towers were finished. Then the two main cables were hung. The main cables were attached to the anchorages and strung between the two towers.

The main cables had to be very strong. They had to carry the weight of the bridge. Each main cable was three feet thick.

Thinner cables were then hung from the main cables. These thinner cables were known as **suspender cables**. They were made of steel rope. The roadway of the bridge was fixed to the suspender cables.

Did You Know?

Each of the main cables is a bundle of 61 smaller cables. The two main cables are each more than a mile long.

Parts of the roadway are hanging from suspender cables.

In 1937 the Golden Gate Bridge was finished!

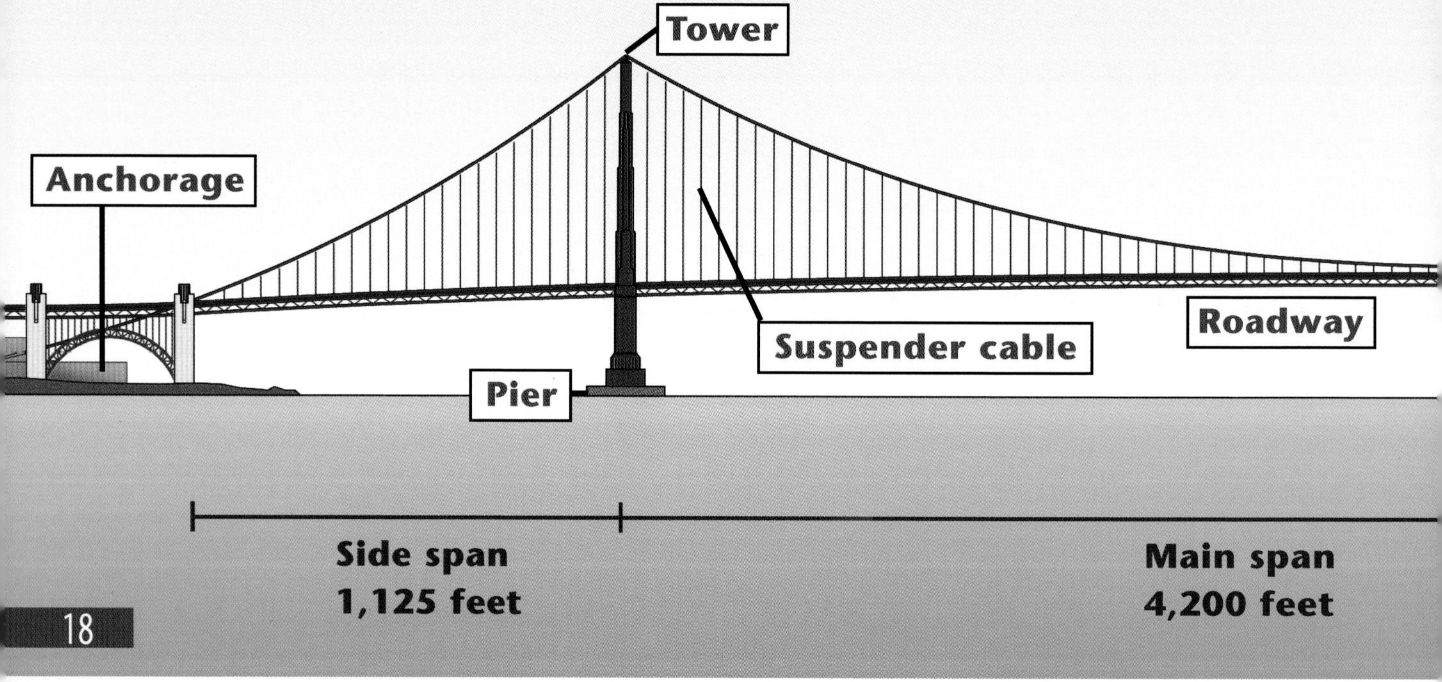

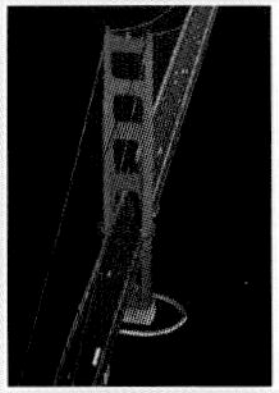

How long is the Golden Gate Bridge?

Is the suspended part of the bridge longer or shorter than a mile?

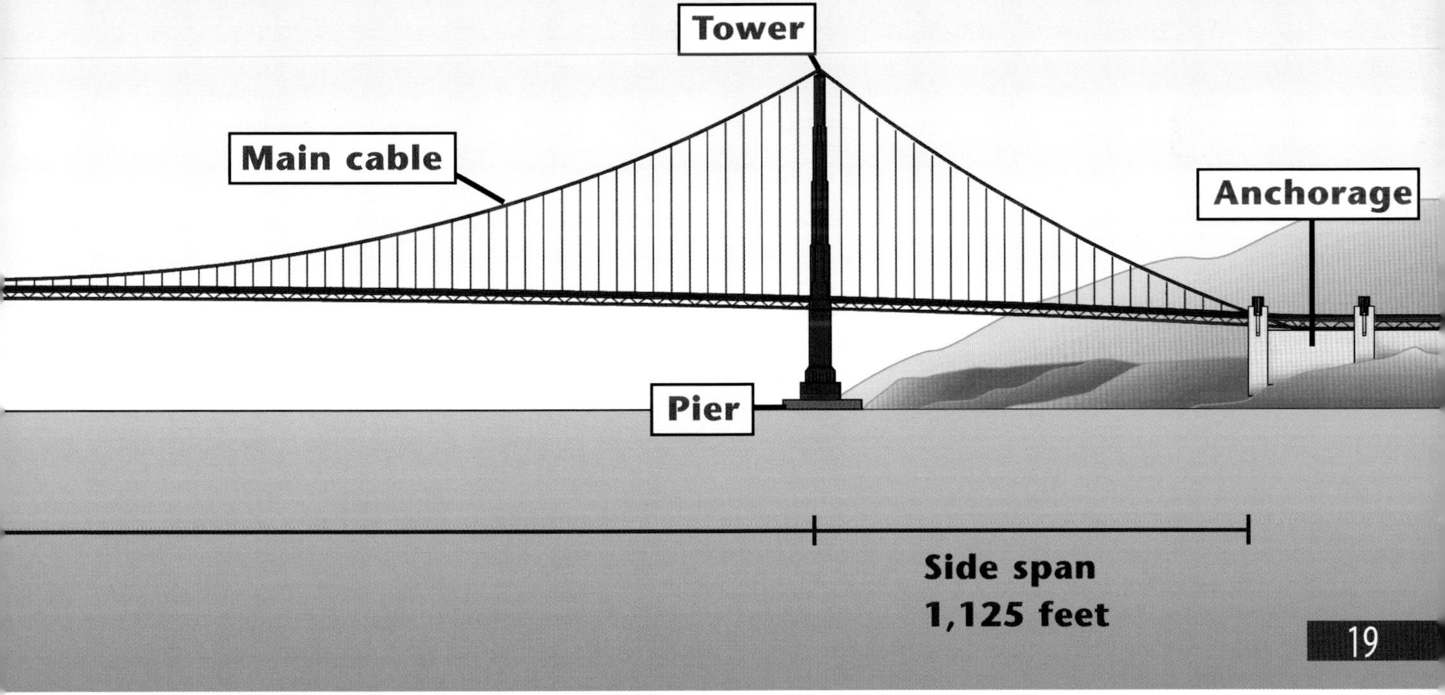

The Bridge: Past and Present

On May 27, 1937, the Golden Gate Bridge was opened. People were allowed to walk on the bridge. Over 200,000 people visited the bridge that day. The next day the bridge was opened to cars.

Thousands of people walked along the Golden Gate Bridge the day it opened.

Did You Know?

The Golden Gate Bridge is one of America's famous landmarks. Every day about 115,000 cars cross the bridge. About how many cars cross the bridge in a week?

Today people use the Golden Gate Bridge to travel easily to and from San Francisco. You can still cross the Golden Gate Strait by boat or ferry—but only if you want to!

The Golden Gate Bridge was once the longest suspension bridge in the world. A few bridges are longer than this one now, but the Golden Gate Bridge is one of the most spectacular!

Glossary

anchorage	huge blocks of concrete that hold the main cables at the end of the bridge
cables	ropes made of steel wires
engineer	a person who plans and builds buildings and bridges
main cables	the cables that hang between the towers on a suspension bridge
peninsula	land surrounded by water on three sides
pier	a base built in water that supports a bridge tower
span	the distance between two ends
suspender cables	the cables that join the main cables to the roadway
suspension bridge	a bridge with a roadway that is held up by cables that hang between two towers

Index

anchorage 12–13, 16, 18–19
arch bridge 11
beam bridge 11
boat 4, 22
cable 9, 10, 12, 16–17, 18–19, 23
cable-stayed bridge 10
engineer 6, 8, 23
ferry 4, 22
Golden Gate Strait 4–5, 6, 14, 22
main cable 9, 12, 16–17, 19, 23
Paine, Clifford E. 8
pier 4, 14, 16, 18–19, 23
roadway 16–17, 18
San Francisco 3, 4, 12, 22
Strauss, Joseph B. 6–7, 8–9, 10, 12
suspender cable 16–17, 18, 23
suspension bridge 9, 10, 22, 23
tower 8–9, 10, 12, 14–15, 16, 18–19